Red, White, Blue, AND Uncle Who?
The Stories behind Some of America's Patriotic Symbols

BY TERESA BATEMAN

ILLUSTRATED BY

JOHN O'BRIEN

Holiday House / New York

In memory of Great-Grandpa Charlie,
who taught me to sing "She's a Grand Old Flag"
when I was very young
T. B.

For Tess
J. O.

Text copyright © 2001 by Teresa Bateman
Art copyright © 2001 by John O'Brien
All Rights Reserved
Printed in the United States of America
www.holidayhouse.com

Library of Congress Cataloging-in-Publication Data
Bateman, Teresa.
Red, white, blue, and Uncle who? : the stories behind some of America's patriotic symbols
/ by Teresa Bateman ; illustrated by John O'Brien.—1st ed.
p. cm.
Includes bibliographical references and index.
ISBN 0-8234-1285-7 (hardcover)
ISBN 0-8234-1784-0 (paperback)
1. Emblems, National—United States—Juvenile literature.
[1. Emblems, National. 2. National monuments.] I. O'Brien, John, 1953– II. Title
JC346 .B37 2001
929.9—dc21   00-057258

ISBN-13: 978-0-8234-1285-3 (hardcover)   ISBN-10: 0-8234-1285-7 (hardcover)
ISBN-13: 978-0-8234-1784-1 (paperback)   ISBN-10: 0-8234-1784-0 (paperback)

Contents

No one is certain who sewed the first American flag. Legend says it was Betsy Ross. Her grandson, William J. Canby, claimed that in June 1776, George Washington, Robert Morris, and George Ross visited Mrs. Ross in Philadelphia. They asked Mrs. Ross to make a flag from a rough drawing. Mrs. Ross suggested using a five-pointed star and showed how it could easily be cut from a piece of folded cloth. Most experts agree that while Betsy Ross did make American flags, she probably did not design the first one. The only documented claim to the first design was from Francis Hopkinson, a signer of the Declaration of Independence. A bill he submitted to Congress asked that he be paid for designing the United States Flag. After careful consideration Congress denied the bill, stating that Mr. Hopkinson was not the sole designer of the flag. It seems likely the flag was designed by committee.

Changes in the nation brought changes to the flag. A new star and a new stripe were added for each new state that joined the Union. The country was growing rapidly, and adding so many stars and stripes soon became a problem. On January 13, 1794, Congress passed a second flag resolution. It stated that, beginning May 1, 1795, the flag should be "fifteen stripes, alternate red and white," with a union of "fifteen stars, white on a blue field." A fifteen-stripe flag flew over Fort McHenry in 1814, inspiring Francis Scott Key's "The Star-Spangled Banner."

By 1817 the nation was much larger than fifteen states. The flag was cluttered with twenty stars and stripes. As part of the Flag Act of 1818, Congress decided the flag should return to thirteen horizontal red and white stripes representing the thirteen original colonies. A new star, but no stripe, would be added on the Fourth of July following each new state's admission to the Union.

When southern states seceded from the Union prior to the Civil War, flag makers were faced with a dilemma. They had added stars for each new state. Should they subtract stars for states that seceded? Many angry Northerners thought that an excellent idea. President Abraham Lincoln did not agree. He was determined to hold the Union together. Throughout the Civil War (from 1861–65), Union troops marched under a flag containing all of its stars. In fact, a new star was added when West Virginia became a state in 1863. Soon both North and South were flying the same flag again.

President William Howard Taft issued orders to standardize flags in 1912. These specified flag measurements and star placement, and included instructions that flags should be used until worn out, then suitably retired.

Eleven years later, on June 14, 1923, leaders from sixty-eight patriotic groups met in Washington, D.C., to draw up a set of rules outlining the proper handling of the United States flag. In 1942, Congress put all of these rules into The Flag Code, which became law. The Flag Code gives correct ratios for all parts of the flag and provides rules and directions for correctly handling the flag so that it is always treated with respect. The federal Flag Code is updated when necessary, most recently in 1976.

Flag Vocabulary

canton: The top inner quarter of the flag; on the
   U.S. flag, the blue area with the stars (also called the union).
field: The main body of the flag.
fly: The bottom, or length, of the flag.
halyard: The rope or cord used to raise and lower the flag.
hoist: The flag's side, or width.

Some Flag Code Rules

- The flag must be raised swiftly, but lowered slowly.
- Do not fly a flag in bad weather unless it is an all-weather flag.
- The flag may be flown at night only if properly lighted.
- The flag should never touch the ground.
- In the United States no other flag may be flown higher than the American flag except at United Nations headquarters, where it is flown at the same level as the flags of other nations.

- When a government leader or important person dies, the flag is often flown at half-staff. To correctly place a flag at half-staff, first raise it to the top, then lower it to the halfway position. Before lowering the flag at night, it should first be raised to the top.
- The flag may be flown upside down only when very great danger exists. This is considered a distress signal.
- The United States flag is folded into a triangle to symbolize the shape of the tricorn hats worn by soldiers of the Revolutionary War.

The Great Seal

Take out a dollar bill and look at it closely. George Washington smiles at you from the front, but what are those weird designs on the back? The two circles on the back of the dollar bill show the two sides of the Great Seal of the United States. The front of this seal is used on all official documents and treaties.

The Continental Congress commissioned the designing of a seal right after the Declaration of Independence was signed on July 4, 1776. The final design was adopted by Congress on June 20, 1782.

The Great Seal of the United States is a round piece of metal cast on both sides. The secretary of state keeps it to use on official documents, but only by the order of the president of the United States. On the front is a bald eagle, wings spread, with the shield of the United States across its chest. This shield has thirteen red and white vertical stripes for the original thirteen colonies. The shield stands on the eagle's chest without support, showing that the United States relies on itself, and its own virtue, for right and justice. The top of the shield, a horizontal blue stripe, represents Congress. In one talon the eagle holds the olive branches of peace. In the other it clutches the arrows of war. In its beak the eagle holds a ribbon, upon which are written the Latin words *E pluribus unum,* which mean "From many, one": From many states, one nation arose. Above the eagle's head is a circular cloud filled with thirteen five-pointed stars. These represent "a glory, or, breaking through a cloud."

The back of the seal contains a thirteen-layer pyramid, the layers standing for the original thirteen colonies. The stone of the pyramid represents lasting strength. On the bottom layer of stone is the Roman numeral date MDCCLXXVI—1776, the date of the Declaration of Independence. The pyramid is capped by a large eye in a triangle to represent the all-seeing eye of Divine Providence. Above the triangle are the Latin words *Annuit coeptis*—"He [God] has favored our undertaking." Below the pyramid are the Latin words *Novus ordo seclorum*—"A new order of the ages [is created]."

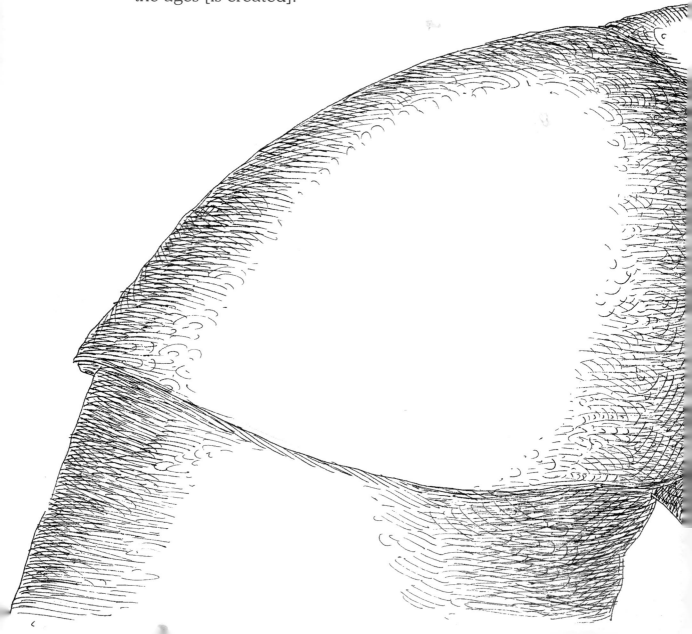

15

The Liberty Bell

In 1751 the Pennsylvania Assembly decided to purchase a bell for the Pennsylvania State House in Philadelphia to celebrate the colony's fiftieth anniversary. They ordered the bell from London, England.

Nine months later, when the large bell was unloaded in the State House yard, there was great excitement. It was hung on a temporary frame and everyone held their breath to hear its majestic ring. When the clapper struck, people gasped. Instead of a golden tone, there was a horrible clanking. A wide crack had opened on the curved bell.

Two local men, John Pass and John Stow, said they could fix the bell. It was broken into small pieces with sledgehammers, melted down, then recast with the addition of some copper for strength. In March of 1753 the new bell was ready. The rope was pulled, the clapper swung, and people hushed so that they could hear the bell's beautiful tones. Unfortunately, the sound that emerged was harsh and dull. Pass and Stow took the bell down, melted it again, and added tin to improve the tone. When the bell was rung on June 7, 1753, everyone agreed that it was improved with the tin, but it still didn't give out the desired mellow, rich sound. Still, it was rung as the State House bell and petitions from irritated neighbors were ignored.

At the beginning of the Revolutionary War, Pennsylvania hosted the Second Continental Congress. The Declaration of Independence was debated, then ratified, at the State House. On July 8, 1776, when the new Declaration was first read aloud to the

people, the State House bell rang out for liberty. Suddenly the inscription on the bell—"Proclaim Liberty Throughout All the Land unto All the Inhabitants Thereof. Leviticus XXV:X"—gained new meaning.

During the Revolutionary War the bell was concealed under the floor of a church in a nearby town to prevent the British from melting it down for ammunition. When the British left Philadelphia in June 1778, the bell was returned. Thereafter the State House bell was rung every July Fourth and on state occasions. In 1781 it rang to announce Great Britain's surrender at Yorktown. It rang again when the peace treaty was signed in 1783. When the new Constitution was approved in 1788, the bell rang out to announce the news.

When the nation's capital moved from Philadelphia to Washington, D.C., the bell stayed behind. It was still used for special occasions. On July 8, 1835, the bell was rung to note the passing of Chief Justice of the Supreme Court John Marshall. To everyone's horror, the bell cracked. The Philadelphia City Council ordered a new bell and offered to throw in the old one as scrap metal. However, it would have been expensive to haul the old bell away, so the bell maker refused to take it.

In 1846 a newspaper writer remembered the old bell and suggested it be rung to celebrate George Washington's birthday. Suddenly the bell was famous again. People called it the Liberty Bell. Its crack was drilled and widened to keep the edges from vibrating against each other. On February 22, 1846, George Washington's birthday, it began ringing. At midday, however, the crack widened even farther. Impossible to repair, the Liberty Bell became useless as a bell and the clapper was removed.

The United States soon neared its hundredth anniversary. People began remembering places that had played a role in the nation's birth. The Pennsylvania State House became known as Independence Hall. The Liberty Bell was placed on display there. In January 1976, as part of the celebration of the nation's bicentennial, the bell was moved to its own glass pavilion across the street from Independence Hall.

The bell still rings, very gently, for freedom. It is tapped with a mallet for special events and annually on the Fourth of July.

"The Star-Spangled Banner"

The Americans had won the Revolutionary War, but new issues soon arose between the United States and Great Britain. The War of 1812 resulted, lasting from 1812 to 1815.

In August of 1814, British troops landed, marched on Washington, D.C., and burned the capital. The British soldiers returned to their ships, planning to land next along Chesapeake Bay and set up a base from which they could send troops north. At the same time there were plans for an army from Canada to make its way south. The key was Baltimore, and the key to Baltimore lay in Chesapeake Bay—Fort McHenry.

The commander of Fort McHenry, Major George Armistead, had ordered a huge flag—measuring 42 feet long by 30 feet high. This he raised over the fort, saying he wanted it so big that "the British will have no trouble seeing it from a distance." It was made by Mrs. Mary Young Pickersgill of Baltimore and her thirteen-year-old daughter. The stars measured two feet from point to point, and the stripes were two feet wide.

On September 13, 1814, Fort McHenry's flag was whipping in the breeze as the fort was attacked by sixteen British ships. On the deck of a ship in Chesapeake Bay stood Francis Scott Key, a young American lawyer.

Key had come aboard the H.M.S. *Tonnant* with Colonel J. S. Skinner to seek the release of Dr. William Beanes, an elderly

physician taken captive by the British. Dr. Beanes was released when Key and Skinner produced evidence that the doctor had treated both British and American soldiers. During these negotiations, the Americans had learned of the British plans for invading Baltimore. Skinner, Key, and Beanes were forced to wait out the battle behind enemy lines.

The first shot was fired on Fort McHenry at 6:00 A.M. on September 13. The attack continued without letup. During the day Key and his companions watched the battle. That night Key paced the decks, observing as the battle raged, unsure which side would be victorious.

British ships fired 200-pound bombshells that were supposed to explode upon reaching their targets. Undependable, they often exploded in midair instead. By their light, and by the light of the rockets that were also being fired, Key could see the flag still flying over the fort.

It began to rain. Soon it was impossible to see anything. Key, Skinner, and Beanes waited. As long as the noise continued, they knew Fort McHenry had not surrendered.

It was early morning when the noise suddenly ceased. A heavy fog crept in. The battle must have been over, but who had won? When the sun finally rose and the fog lifted, the three men saw, to their joy, the American flag, still flying over Fort McHenry. The British were retreating!

Taking out an envelope from a letter he had started to write, Francis Scott Key tried to put down his feelings in a poem. He worked on the poem during his journey back to shore and in his hotel room that night. The next day he took a copy of the four verses to his brother-in-law, Judge Joseph H. Nicholson.

Judge Nicholson immediately sent it to the printer and asked that copies be distributed throughout the city. The poem, called "Defense of Fort McHenry," also included instructions that it might be sung to the tune of "To Anacreon in Heaven," a popular song of the time. On September 20 the poem appeared in a Baltimore newspaper as well. The song quickly spread. Soon everyone was singing it.

In 1916 President Woodrow Wilson ordered that "The Star-Spangled Banner," as it had come to be known, be played at all state occasions. In 1931, after numerous petitions, the United States Congress named this song our national anthem. The original star-spangled banner that flew over Fort McHenry is now in the Smithsonian Institution.

Uncle Sam

While there is some dispute about the origin of Uncle Sam, many experts trace it back to a man named Sam Wilson.

Samuel Wilson was born in what later became Arlington, Massachusetts, on September 13, 1766. He was the seventh of thirteen children and came from a family of patriots. In 1789 Sam moved to Troy, New York, and started a meat-packing business. He was tall and lean, with long gray hair but no beard, and he stood out in a crowd. Many of his brothers and sisters, with their large families, settled in the area as well, so a troop of local children called him Uncle Sam. Soon the nickname spread and was used by friends and family alike.

When the War of 1812 began, Wilson's company supplied salt pork and beef to the army. Wilson also became a meat inspector. Both the barrels that he inspected and those from his factory were stamped U.S. At the time, *U. States* commonly stood for "United States." The new initials confused people. When asked what *U.S.* stood for, some of the workers at his factory joked that the initials meant "Uncle Sam" Wilson. This became a common joke.

Soldiers began calling themselves "Uncle Sam's Army," and their rations "Uncle Sam's meat." Soon all government property stamped with the initials was said to be Uncle Sam's. Today, Uncle Sam is a nickname for the entire United States government.

The cartoon character of Uncle Sam, with red-white-and-blue suit, appeared in political cartoons in the 1830s. His hat and beard were added after the Civil War. Some say Uncle Sam's beard was inspired by Abraham Lincoln's.

Congress adopted Uncle Sam as a national symbol in 1961.

The Statue of Liberty

At a dinner party in France in 1865, the talk turned to the tragic death of President Abraham Lincoln. Many French citizens felt a monument was needed to show France's support of the United States and honor liberty. Perhaps France could present such a monument for the one hundredth anniversary of the signing of the Declaration of Independence, in 1876.

At the party was Frédéric-Auguste Bartholdi, a sculptor. In 1870 he made his first small clay model of a woman representing

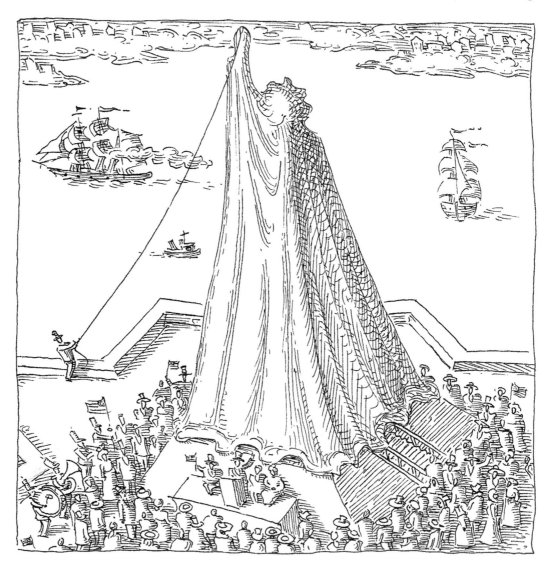

liberty. A year later he traveled to America and saw Bedloe Island in Upper New York Bay, the home of star-shaped Fort Wood. Bartholdi felt it would be the perfect place for his statue.

In 1875 France began raising money for the statue. In 1876, at a studio in Paris, Bartholdi began constructing it. His mother's face inspired the head, while the body was modeled by Jeanne-Émilie Baheux de Puysieux, who eventually became Bartholdi's wife. Taller than a fourteen-story building, the statue needed to be easily assembled and disassembled—light enough to move, but heavy enough to stand firm in a storm. Above all, it had to be beautiful. Finally Bartholdi hit upon a solution—he would use thin copper plates attached to a solid iron frame.

The statue had to be assembled outdoors. Bartholdi built plaster models in different sizes. Carpenters created wooden molds. Copper sheets were placed into these molds and coppersmiths noisily hammered them into shape. Once the penny-thin copper was ready, it was riveted into place on an iron framework designed by Alexandre-Gustave Eiffel, the same man who would engineer the Eiffel Tower.

A formal ceremony was held in 1884 to present the statue to representatives of the U.S. government. The next year it was taken apart and packed into more than two hundred cases for shipment to America.

While the people of France were footing the bill for the statue, the United States was expected to pay for its pedestal, the property on which it would stand, and installation costs. Joseph Pulitzer, owner and editor of the New York *World,* became involved, giving the fund drive needed publicity.

On August 5, 1884, a 6-ton granite block was laid on Bedloe Island within the star-shaped walls that were all that remained of Fort Wood. This block would be the cornerstone of the statue's pedestal.

The Statue of Liberty arrived in New York in mid-June 1885. Gradually the statue rose over New York Harbor. When the torch was put in place, two rows of holes were cut into the flame and covered with glass plates so that an electric light could shine through.

On October 28, 1886, President Grover Cleveland was scheduled to dedicate the statue. Bartholdi and his wife traveled from France for the occasion. The day of the dedication dawned windy and rainy, but the weather did not deter huge crowds from watching the biggest parade New York City had ever seen.

After the parade many people took to boats to watch the rest of the ceremony. Only a select group were allowed on the island. Of these only two or three were women. It was common at the time to exclude women from public events, but members of the suffragette movement did not take the snub tamely. Some of the more militant women rented a boat and sailed near the island. Their shouts disrupted the speeches as they pointed out that the statue being honored was a woman, but were she alive she would be unable to vote in either the United States or France.

At the base of the statue, speakers gathered. Bartholdi was in the crown of the statue, ready to pull the cord that would release the French flag veiling the statue's eyes. He awaited only a signal from the ground.

The ceremony began. However, William M. Evarts, president of the American Committee, never got a chance to give the long speech he had planned. When he paused for emphasis just a few minutes into his speech, the signal to unveil the statue was accidentally given.

The crowd roared, horns blew, and bells rang as the Statue of Liberty was revealed to all.

The statue was immediately popular. People from all over the world came to visit Lady Liberty.

In 1924 the Statue of Liberty and Liberty Island were declared a national monument by President Calvin Coolidge. Nearby Ellis Island became part of the Statue of Liberty National Monument in 1965.

The Statue of Liberty, from 1984–1986, was completely renovated. Iron was replaced with stainless steel in the statue's interior and the old flame was completely replaced with a new one made from copper with gold plating. Today people from many nations travel to the United States. Many of those who visit New York City take the ferry from Manhattan to Liberty Island. There they can appreciate Bartholdi's masterpiece as they read the words from Emma Lazarus from the poem "The New Colossus" that celebrates those who have come from other lands to make the United States their home. The poem ends:

Give me your tired,
your poor,
Your huddled masses
yearning to breathe free,
The wretched refuse
of your teeming shore.
Send these, the homeless,
tempest-tost, to me,
I lift my lamp beside
the golden door!

Mount Rushmore

The idea for Mount Rushmore was first suggested by Doane Robinson in 1924. As secretary of the South Dakota Historical Society, he thought huge carvings of famous people from the Wild West would lure tourists to his state. Sculptor John Gutzon de la Mothe Borglum, who was carving an enormous panorama featuring heroes of the South on a granite cliff at Stone Mountain in Georgia, seemed perfect for the job.

Borglum went to the Black Hills in the summer of 1925, looking for a site for the carving. When he saw Mount Rushmore, a granite cliff 400 feet high and 1,000 feet long, he knew he'd found the perfect place.

Borglum decided to carve four presidents. Washington was chosen for his role in creating the Constitution; Jefferson, for the Declaration of Independence and the Louisiana Purchase; Lincoln, for leading the country through a civil war that nearly divided it; and Theodore Roosevelt, the most controversial face, for his part in creating the Panama Canal, which linked two oceans. Roosevelt had been dead only six years and many felt his contributions were insignificant. In 1927 President Calvin Coolidge dedicated the memorial, and work began.

Some were not pleased. Many Sioux Indians felt the sculpture, which was to stand on their sacred grounds, was sacrilege. There were others who felt it would be an eyesore or environmentally unsound.

The original plan called for carving the presidents down to their waists. This was dropped when the granite lower on the mountain proved unsuitable for carving. Borglum's artistry created a national monument, but other men did the hard labor. The work was difficult, but no worker was killed or permanently injured while carving Mount Rushmore.

Workers were lowered in special leather seats with steel frames and two safety straps. Much of the stone was removed with dynamite, followed by drills and pneumatic hammers. It took fourteen years to remove almost half a million tons of granite from the cliff to create the 50- to 70-foot-high faces.

First to be carved was George Washington. This head was dedicated on July 4, 1930. The Jefferson head was dedicated on

August 30, 1936. Lincoln followed Jefferson and was dedicated on September 17, 1937, to celebrate the anniversary of the signing of the Constitution. Last on the mountain was Theodore Roosevelt, dedicated July 2, 1939. On October 31, 1941, work on the mountain ended.

Today Mount Rushmore is a national treasure. The days of carving huge memorials are not over, however. Nearby in the Black Hills, another huge monument is being blasted from stone. It pays homage to Native Americans and shows Oglala Sioux chief Crazy Horse mounted and riding into the wind.

The White House

The official residence of the president of the United States is the White House, located at 1600 Pennsylvania Avenue in Washington, D.C. It has been the home of every president except George Washington. Washington helped choose both the site and design for the house, but his presidency ended before the house was ready. Today the White House is known throughout the world. It is a showcase where world leaders gather, but it hasn't always been so comfortable.

French architect Major Pierre Charles L'Enfant was given the job of designing the new capital in 1791. L'Enfant thought the president of the United States should live like a king in a great palace. Americans had just fought a war to free themselves from a king. Neither they nor Washington thought that this would be appropriate. They preferred a simple, stately house.

In 1792, at the suggestion of Thomas Jefferson, a contest was held asking for designs. Nine were submitted. The winner of the $500 prize was a young architect named James Hoban, from South Carolina, who had the good sense to find out what Washington liked and designed the house accordingly. He even discovered that Washington's guests frequently gathered in an oval around the man; therefore Hoban included an oval room in his design. The President's House was the first major public building built in Washington, D.C.

Construction began on October 13, 1792, with the laying of the cornerstone. For the next eight years building continued, with some slave labor being used. There were a few construction problems. The stones tended to soak up rainwater. It was feared that in

winter the water would freeze and cause the stones to crack. This problem was solved by sealing each stone with whitewash, making the house a stunning white.

John Adams, the second president of the United States, was the first to live in the house. Adams arrived on November 1, 1800. The house was basically complete, but the living quarters were unfinished. It was cold and musty, and there wasn't enough furniture. There were also no nearby wells. Servants had to carry water from a spring nearly a mile and a half away. The yard was a swamp. John Adams was unimpressed.

On the evening of August 24, 1814, during the War of 1812,

British soldiers entered Washington. President James Madison was forced to flee. His wife, Dolley, left as well, but not before rescuing the Declaration of Independence and the life-sized portrait of George Washington painted by Gilbert Stuart.

British soldiers set the President's House ablaze, as well as other buildings in the capital. The smoke could be seen as far away as Baltimore. Fortunately, rain doused the fire. Still, there was extensive damage. Rebuilding of the President's House began in March of 1815 and was finished in 1817. The outside was whitewashed to cover smoke damage. It had been whitewashed in the past, of course, but now the nickname the White House was beginning to stick. In 1901 President Theodore Roosevelt officially established the name by engraving it on his stationery.

In 1902 the three-story Executive Wing was added.

Franklin Delano Roosevelt added a modern kitchen in the 1930s, and his physical disability resulted in the addition of an indoor swimming pool for regular exercise.

By 1948 thirty-one families had called the White House home. Repairs were desperately needed. Some suggested it would cost less to tear down the old building and erect a new one, but the White House had a history that made it worth saving.

The White House was gutted, and the entire interior was rebuilt, more than doubling the number of rooms: from 62 to 132. Fireproofing was added as well. President Harry S. Truman and his family lived across the street in Blair House during the rebuilding. As different families have lived in the White House, they have each left their mark. President Truman was responsible for the addition of a balcony. Jacqueline Bouvier Kennedy completely refurnished the White House in the early 1960s.

In 1964 Lyndon B. Johnson established the Committee for the Preservation of the White House by executive order.

Today the White House sits on just over eighteen acres, surrounded by beautiful gardens. The second floor houses the president and his family. There are also offices and guest rooms. The third floor contains rooms for staff and guests, as well as a solarium. The ground floor has cloakrooms, a kitchen and library, and a china room, as well as formal rooms open to the public. These include the East Room, the oval Blue Room, the Red Room, the Green Room, and the State Dining Room.

There are four entrances to the White House. Generally the north door on 1600 Pennsylvania Avenue is used for state visitors, family, and friends. The south door is for high government officials and foreign diplomats. The west door is used by the president and his staff, and the east door is used by the public.

The Capitol

In 1791 Pierre L'Enfant, city designer, and President George Washington selected a location for the Capitol, then called the Congress House. It was to be on an elevated site known as Jenkins Hill—today's Capitol Hill.

A competition was held to determine the design. William Thornton, a Philadelphia doctor and amateur architect, won $500 and a city lot for his design of a grand building with two wings joined by a central domed rotunda.

On September 18, 1793, the cornerstone of the Congress House was laid by George Washington. Construction, however, was slow. It was hard to find good materials, qualified labor, and adequate funding. Still, in 1800 Congress moved from Philadelphia to its new, unfinished home.

Construction continued until, in 1814, it suffered a major setback when British troops, under the direction of Sir George Cockburn, marched on Washington during the War of 1812. They burned many buildings, including the Capitol. Both wings were set ablaze. Damage could have been worse—a sudden rainstorm put out the fire.

Congress met for several years in another building, the Brick Capitol, while rebuilding took place. Charles Bulfinch supervised the rebuilding.

Five years after the Capitol was burned, the United States Congress moved back in. The new building was not complete, however. It consisted of two wings connected by a domeless center wall. Work on the Rotunda continued slowly.

In 1829 the Capitol was complete. A low wooden dome covered with copper rose over the Rotunda, and the two wings became part of a single, impressive building. However, the nation kept growing and the government grew along with it. Soon it became clear that the building was too small. New extensions to both wings were approved in 1850, and the cornerstone for these was laid in 1851. Enlarging the Capitol, however, would make the low dome appear out of proportion. Congress voted to replace it with a much larger cast-iron dome designed by Thomas U. Walter.

Other construction went on, and soon both the House and the Senate were in their new halls as work continued.

During the Civil War construction on the extensions was suspended. The Capitol was used as a hospital and army barracks, with a bakery and kitchen in the basement. Work on the dome continued; the old Bulfinch dome was taken down and replaced with the more impressive dome. President Abraham Lincoln was criticized for going on with this expensive project during the war, but he considered it vital to continue the work to show that the Union would soon be united again under a central government.

On December 2, 1863, the 19 1/2-foot-tall statue of a woman—*Freedom*—sculpted by Thomas Crawford was raised to its place atop the newly completed Capitol dome. With the new dome, the building looked much as it does today. In 1870 the exteriors of the extensions were completed. The building was finished.

Today the Capitol is a majestic symbol of our nation. Atop Capitol Hill, its white marble walls gleam. The Capitol houses Congress, consisting of the Senate and the House of Representatives, who make the laws by which we live. The northern wing houses the United States Senate, while the House of Representatives meets in the southern wing.

The Rotunda—the domed, circular center of the building—is decorated with statues of famous Americans, artwork illustrating great events in American history, and a beautiful fresco on the inside of the dome.

More changes may be ahead for the Capitol, but it will always stand as a symbol of the government Lincoln described: "of the people, by the people, for the people."

The National Mall

When the location of the new capital of the United States was chosen, President George Washington appointed Pierre Charles L'Enfant to design the city. Part of L'Enfant's vision included a broad band of greenery descending from the Capitol through the heart of the city. Unfortunately, that portion of L'Enfant's plan fell by the wayside as the city grew. Although an attempt was made to turn it into a park, soon the area designed as the National Mall was crisscrossed with railroad lines and a polluted canal. Shanties sprang up here and there on the swampy ground, and animals rooted through garbage dumped there. While some of the grander buildings in the area, including the Washington Monument, were completed and landscaped, the Mall became more and more of an eyesore.

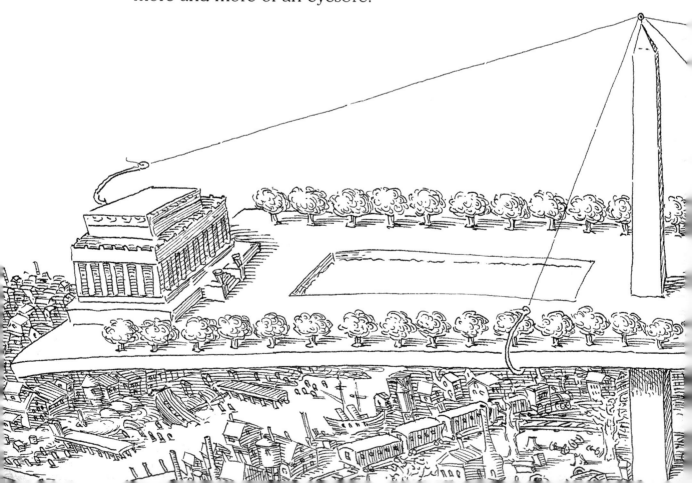

Finally, in 1902, a plan was developed, under Senator James McMillan, to improve the National Mall. It returned to L'Enfant's original design. The railroad was moved, some monuments were relocated, the garbage was cleaned up, landscaping teams moved in, and slowly the site began to improve.

Today the National Mall is a huge open space surrounded by impressive museums. It sweeps down from Capitol Hill to the Washington Monument. Nearby are several other monuments, such as the Vietnam Veterans Memorial, the Thomas Jefferson Memorial, and the Lincoln Memorial. Citizens gather on the Mall for many reasons, both political and recreational. Families picnic; joggers exercise on the paths. It has been the site of festivals as well as demonstrations, including the March on Washington in August of 1963 led by Martin Luther King, Jr. It is truly a place where citizens can gather and appreciate their capital.

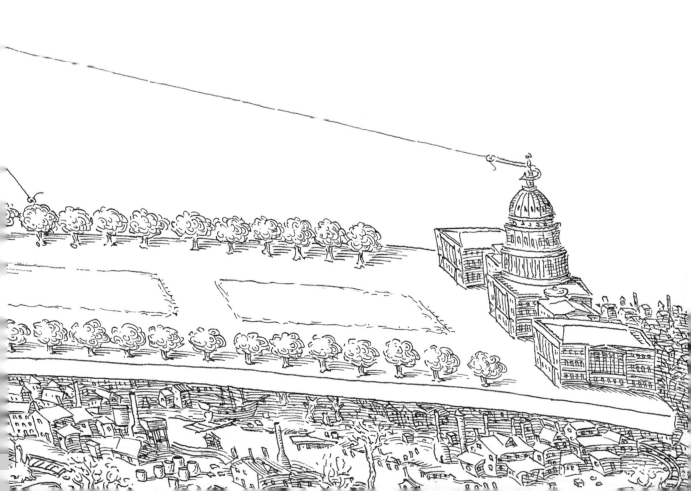

The Washington Monument

George Washington was the commander in chief of the Continental army during the Revolutionary War. He later became the first president of the United States: he was elected in 1788 and reelected in 1792. Much admired for his character, Washington well earned the title Father of His Country. He died on December 14, 1799.

The idea of a specific memorial for George Washington first emerged in August 1783, before he even became president. The Continental Congress at the time resolved that a statue of General George Washington astride a horse should be erected at the place where Congress would eventually reside.

However, planning for a statue and paying for one were two different things. Regardless of the high esteem in which George Washington was held, the funds were simply not available. In fact, it was only after Washington's death that Congress recognized, with some chagrin, that the statue had never been built.

Over the next thirty-four years other memorials were planned, but none was constructed. When would an appropriate memorial to George Washington be built?

In 1836 the Washington National Monument Society held a contest for a design for a fitting memorial to the man who was, according to Henry Lee, "first in war, first in peace, first in the hearts of his countrymen." Robert Mills, an architect, won with his plan for a grandiose building filled with statues and paintings, with columns that would stand 100 feet high. Rising from this impressive building would be an obelisk—a four-sided pillar—that would

soar an additional 500 feet. It was truly awesome.

This elaborate design was simplified throughout the years by a variety of architects. The grand building was discarded until only the hollow obelisk was left.

The government set aside land at the western end of the Mall in Washington, D.C. Donations were sought, and the cornerstone was laid on July 4, 1848, with a splendid ceremony and a crowd of supporters including Congressman Abraham Lincoln. The trowel used at this event was the same one George Washington himself had used to lay the cornerstone of the Capitol building. Construction began immediately, and the monument shot up.

Funds, however, proved insufficient. Work on the monument soon slowed, then halted entirely in 1854. To everyone's embarrassment, the half-finished monument stood in plain view of anyone who visited the capital. During the Civil War cows grazed around it.

It seemed the monument would never be finished. At last, in 1876, the Washington National Monument Society turned over construction to the government. Nearly forty years after the monument was started, it was finally completed. On December 6, 1884, a capstone of solid aluminum was laid. The dedication of the Washington Monument took place on February 21, 1885. The monument was not opened to the public, however, until October 9, 1888.

At the time it was dedicated, the Washington Monument was the world's highest masonry structure. It is 555 feet 5 $1/8$ inches tall, and 55 feet $1 1/2$ inches wide at the base, and tapers to 34 feet 5 $1/2$ inches at the top. There are 897 steps to the observation room, but visitors must use the elevator to get to the top.

The Washington Monument contains 192 memorial stones that

were donated by individuals, organizations, states, and countries to honor George Washington. These stones are set on the interior walls of the monument.

Over time the Washington Monument began to show signs of wear. Renovation began in 1998 and was completed in 2000.

With these repairs the monument stands as a simple memorial to a man who preferred simple things.

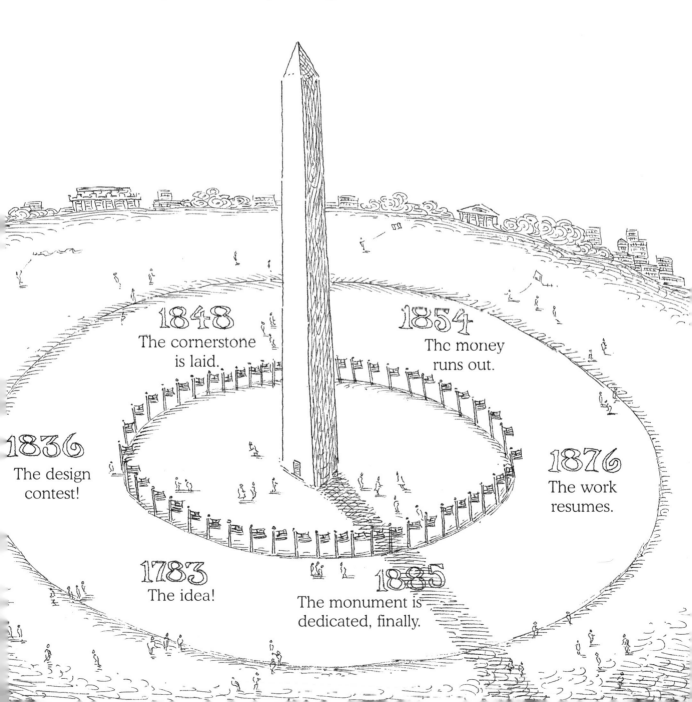

1848
The cornerstone is laid.

1854
The money runs out.

1836
The design contest!

1876
The work resumes.

1783
The idea!

1885
The monument is dedicated, finally.

The Lincoln Memorial

Abraham Lincoln, the sixteenth president of the United States, led the nation through one of its most difficult times—the Civil War, which lasted from 1861 to 1865. This war divided the country over the issues of slavery and states' rights, and Lincoln's leadership is largely credited with uniting it again.

Five days after the Civil War ended, on April 14, 1865, President Lincoln was shot from behind by an actor named John Wilkes Booth. He died on April 15. This assassination shook more than just the United States. People throughout the world mourned the loss of a great man.

Much discussion followed as to a suitable memorial for Abraham Lincoln, but the nation had just been through a devastating war and money was scarce. Not until February 19, 1911, was the Lincoln Memorial Bill signed into law by President William Howard Taft.

On February 12, 1914, work began on the memorial. More than fifty-seven years after Lincoln's death, on Memorial Day, May 30, 1922, 50,000 people gathered for the dedication of the Lincoln Memorial. A small group of veterans from the Civil War sat in places of honor and watched as Chief Justice of the Supreme Court William Howard Taft (who had served as president from 1909 to 1913) presented the Lincoln Memorial to President Warren G. Harding. It was truly an impressive structure.

The Lincoln Memorial stands at the west end of the Mall. It is nearly 80 feet tall, 188 feet long, and $118\,^1/_2$ feet wide; it is surrounded by thirty-six marble columns, representing the states that were in the Union at the time of Lincoln's death. State names are carved above each pillar, along with the dates they entered the Union. Carved above the columns, on the monument's exterior, are the names of the forty-eight states in existence when the memorial was dedicated. A plaque has been added to the memorial commemorating the additions of Alaska and Hawaii. The columns in the memorial are not perfectly straight. They are slightly tilted to avoid an optical illusion that would make the memorial seem crooked.

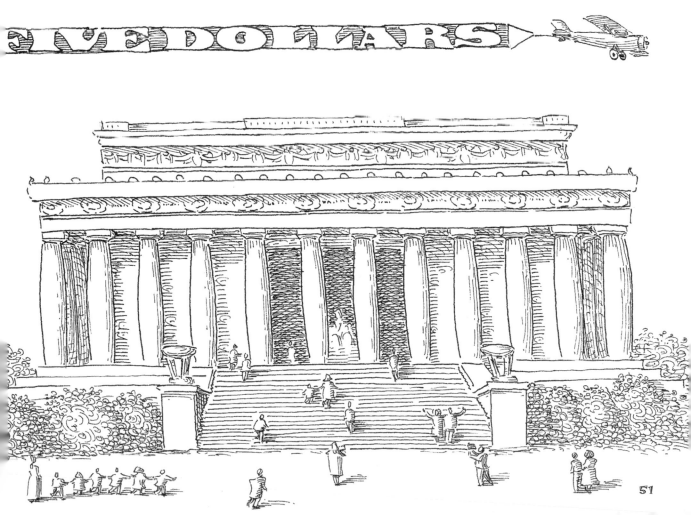

The floor is made of Tennessee pink marble. In the ceiling, panels of 1-inch-thick Alabama marble, soaked in paraffin, allow some light to shine through. Inside the memorial, columns separate it into three parts.

In the main chamber sits a 19-foot-tall statue of Abraham Lincoln, designed by Daniel Chester French out of white Georgia marble. It rests on a pedestal that is 11 feet high. On the north wall Lincoln's Second Inaugural Address is engraved, with a mural by Jules Guerin titled *Reunion* above it. On the south wall is engraved Lincoln's Gettysburg Address. Above it, Guerin's mural *Emancipation* depicts an angel granting freedom to a slave. Stairs lead down to a gallery on the building's south side that contains photographs and portraits of Abraham Lincoln from different times in his life.

The memorial has been the site of many important national events. On Easter Sunday, April 9, 1939, African-American singer Marian Anderson sang there at the invitation of Eleanor Roosevelt, after having been denied permission to sing at Constitution Hall. On August 28, 1963, the March on Washington ended at the Lincoln Memorial. It was there that Martin Luther King, Jr., gave his "I Have a Dream" speech.

More than a million people a year visit the Lincoln Memorial, which is now part of Potomac Park, administered by the U.S. National Park Service. Its quiet marble hall gives people a chance to reflect upon the principles of democracy that made this nation possible, and upon a man who, literally, gave his life for those principles. As is carved in marble: "In this temple, as in the hearts of the people for whom he saved the Union, the memory of Abraham Lincoln is enshrined forever."

The Vietnam Veterans Memorial

When communist guerrillas in South Vietnam tried to overthrow their government, they sparked a conflict that soon escalated into a war between North and South Vietnam. Eventually other nations, including the United States, became involved. The Vietnam War lasted from the 1950s to April 30, 1975, and cost the lives of nearly 60,000 Americans.

The war was unpopular in the United States, and demonstrations against it were common. Returning soldiers were not always honored as heroes and were sometimes subject to ridicule. It wasn't until November 1982 that a memorial to those who gave their lives in the Vietnam War was dedicated.

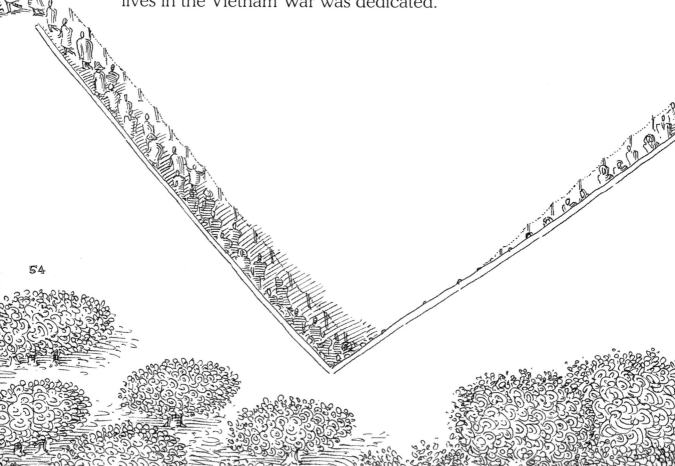

The Vietnam Veterans Memorial began with Jan Scruggs, who served and was wounded in Vietnam. He started the Vietnam Veterans Memorial fund with money earned from the sale of a piece of property. The memorial was entirely paid for by private contributions.

On July 1, 1980, President Jimmy Carter signed a bill authorizing the building of a memorial on public grounds in Washington, D.C. The site would be near the Lincoln Memorial in Constitution Gardens.

A contest, open to all Americans, was held to come up with a design. The prize was $20,000. The only restrictions were that the memorial had to contain the names of all Americans killed or missing in action in the war, harmonize with its location, and not make a political statement about the war. One thousand four hundred and twenty-one designs were submitted. The winner sur-

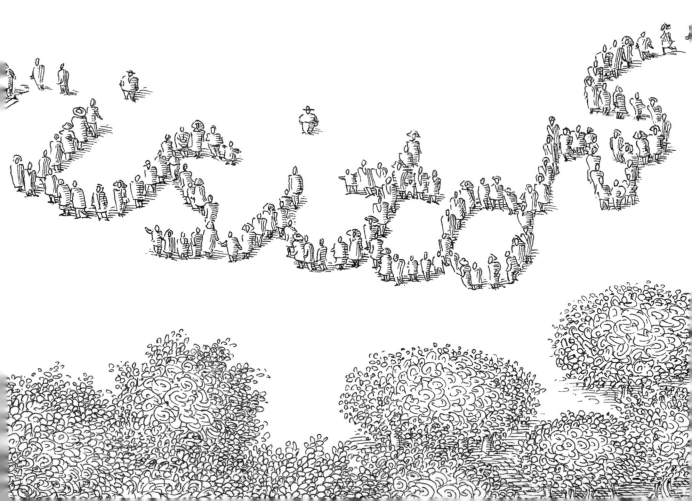

prised everyone. It was from a twenty-one-year-old student from Yale named Maya Ying Lin. She created the design originally as a homework assignment, for which she received a B.

The simple design consists of a stone wall inscribed with the names of those who are dead or still missing from the Vietnam War. The wall is nearly 500 feet long, made from black Indian granite. The names, sandblasted into the granite, are listed chronologically in the order in which they became casualties. Beside each name is a diamond or a cross. Diamonds signify a death, while a cross indicates the person is still missing. Crosses can be changed to diamonds if the person is confirmed dead, or a circle can be drawn around the cross if persons are confirmed alive. Changes are made, as necessary, to the list of names. The wall forms a wide V and is sunk into the earth. The black granite stands out starkly and reflects the land and sky, as well as the faces of those visiting the memorial.

The Vietnam Veterans Memorial was dedicated in November 1982. An estimated 150,000 people were in attendance. Many had served in Vietnam. Others had lost loved ones there.

In 1984 a 7-foot-high statue of three soldiers and a flag designed by Frederick Hart were added to the Vietnam Veterans Memorial. In 1993 the Vietnam Women's Memorial, by sculptor Glenna Goodacre, was added, commemorating the contributions of women veterans.

The Wall provides a place where people can find comfort. Many leave flowers, photographs, medals, and other mementos there, as if the Wall were a grave they wish to decorate.

Part of the Wall's inscription reads as follows:

In honor of the men and women of the armed forces of the United States who served in the Vietnam War. The names of those who gave their lives and of those who remain missing are inscribed in the order they were taken from us.

Our Nation honors the courage, sacrifice and devotion to duty and country of its Vietnam veterans.

The Korean War Memorial

Considered one of the bloodiest wars in history, the Korean War lasted from June 1950 to July 1953. While it started as a conflict between North and South Korea, twenty other nations, including the United States, became involved. Many American soldiers were recalled to active duty, while others were drafted.

The war lasted only a little more than three years, but battle conditions were severe and casualties were heavy. Nearly 54,000 Americans lost their lives in the conflict.

While war memorials were common for veterans of previous wars, the Korean conflict rightly earned the nickname The Forgotten

War. It was over thirty years after the cease-fire before Congress announced legislation for a Korean War Veterans Memorial.

Located in Washington, D.C., across the reflecting pool from the Vietnam Veteran's Memorial, the Korean War Memorial features a triangular garden within a grove of trees. There a silent patrol of nineteen larger-than-life steel soldiers wearing ponchos move up a slight hill where an American flag awaits. The soldiers are loaded down with communications gear and weapons. They represent the different branches of the armed services that fought in Korea.

A black granite wall runs alongside the column of ghost gray soldiers. Upon it are sandblasted 2,400 faces, taken from actual photographs, of men and women who served in this war as support troops. Silently they gaze out at the ghostly platoon.

When the memorial was dedicated in 1995, thousands of Korean War veterans attended the ceremony. The afternoon was

hot, and the evening brought a thunderstorm, but they were not deterred. Some gazed in silence and wept. Others found lost friends and shared the moment. Many brought their children. At last their sacrifice had been acknowledged. As the memorial states:

Our nation honors her uniformed sons and daughters
Who answered their country's call to defend a country
They did not know and a people they had never met.

Freedom Is Not Free.

The Thomas Jefferson Memorial

Thomas Jefferson was the third president of the United States. Possibly more importantly, he is credited with writing the document that set the thirteen colonies on the path to becoming a nation: the Declaration of Independence. On June 26, 1934, Congress created a commission to direct the building of the Thomas Jefferson Memorial.

The site, directly south of the White House and overlooking the Tidal Basin, was chosen in 1937. The architecture for the monument was adapted from plans by John Russell Pope. He took into account Jefferson's own tastes, including his love of the Roman pantheon design. The memorial is an open rotunda, a circular marble building with a domed ceiling surrounded by twenty-six columns. In the center stands a 19-foot-tall bronze statue of Jefferson, created by Rudolph Evans, facing north to the White House. Surrounding the statue, on the interior walls, are carved excerpts from Jefferson's most famous writings, while above the entrance is a sculpture of the Declaration Committee.

The memorial was dedicated on April 13, 1943: the two hundredth anniversary of Jefferson's birth. President Franklin Delano Roosevelt was the main speaker at the dedication.

Not everyone was pleased with the design of the memorial. Some even called it Jefferson's Muffin when it was first built.

Today, however, it is acknowledged as one of the most moving monuments in Washington, D.C. Few can stand surrounded by those marble columns and read the words

"We hold these truths to be self-evident, that all men are created equal . . ."

without realizing the vision of the man and his impact on a nation.

Index